THIS WALKER BOOK BELONGS TO:

_____   ⌊

_____

_____

running

painting

looking

drinking

bouncing

counting

sitting

bending

scowling

digging

smiling

hugging

sweeping

bouncing

stamping

reading

crawling

sucking

For Jack

First published 1993 by Walker Books Ltd
87 Vauxhall Walk, London SE11 5HJ

This edition published 2004

2 4 6 8 10 9 7 5 3 1

© 1993 Shirley Hughes

The right of Shirley Hughes to be identified as
author/illustrator of this work has been asserted by her in
accordance with the Copyright, Designs and Patents Act 1988

This book has been typeset in Plantin

Printed in China

British Library Cataloguing in Publication Data:
a catalogue record for this book is available from the British Library

ISBN 1-84428-470-0

www.walkerbooks.co.uk

Bouncing

Shirley Hughes

WALKER BOOKS
AND SUBSIDIARIES
LONDON · BOSTON · SYDNEY · AUCKLAND

When I throw my big shiny ball...

it bounces away from me.

Bounce, bounce, bounce, bounce!

Then it rolls along the ground, then it stops.

I like bouncing too. In the mornings
I bounce on my bed,

and the baby bounces in his cot.

Mum and Dad's big bed is an even better
place to bounce.

But Dad doesn't much like being bounced

on in the early morning.

So we roll on the floor instead, and the
baby bounces on ME!

After breakfast he
does some dancing
in his baby-bouncer,

and I do some dancing
to the radio.

At my play-group there are big cushions on
the floor where lots of children
can bounce together.

And at home there's a big sofa where we can bounce when Mum isn't looking.

Grandpa and I know a good bouncing game.

I ride on his knees and we sing:

This is the way the ladies ride: trit-trot, trit-trot;

This is the way the gentlemen ride: tarran, tarran;

This is the way the farmers ride: clip-clop, clip-clop;

This is the way the jockeys ride: gallopy, gallopy,

and FALL OFF!

I like bouncing.

I bounce about all day…

bounce, bounce,
bounce, bounce!

Until in the end I stop
bouncing,

and go off to sleep.

running

painting

looking

drinking

bouncing

counting

sitting

bending

scowling

digging

smiling

hugging

sweeping

bouncing

stamping

reading

crawling

sucking

WALKER BOOKS is the world's leading
independent publisher of children's books.
Working with the best authors and illustrators
we create books for all ages, from babies
to teenagers – books your child will
grow up with and always remember. So…

FOR THE BEST CHILDREN'S BOOKS,
LOOK FOR THE BEAR